To..

From..

OTHER MINI GIFTBOOKS IN THIS SERIES:

Welcome to the New Baby
To a very special Aunt
To a very special Daughter
To a very special Grandmother
To a very special Mother-in-law
To a very special Grandpa
Happy Anniversary
To my very special Love
To a very special Mother
To a very special Son
To a very special Dad

To a very special Friend
To a very special Granddaughter
Wishing you Happiness
To my very special Husband
Merry Christmas
To a very special Sister
To my very special Wife
To someone very special Happy
    Birthday
Wishing You The Best Birthday
    Ever

Published simultaneously in 1998 by Exley Publications LLC in the
USA and Exley Publications Ltd in Great Britain.

12 11 10 9 8 7 6 5 4 3 2 1

Copyright © Helen Exley 1998
ISBN 1-85015-931-9

A copy of the CIP data is available from the British Library on request.
All rights reserved. No part of this publication may be reproduced or
transmitted in any form or by any means, electronic or mechanical,
including photocopy, recording or any information storage and retrieval
system without permission in writing from the Publisher.

Edited and words selected by Helen Exley
Illustrated by Juliette Clarke
Printed and bound in Hungary

Exley Publications Ltd, 16 Chalk Hill, Watford, Herts WD1 4BN, UK.
Exley Publications LLC, 232 Madison Avenue, Suite 1206,
NY 10016, USA.

'TO A VERY SPECIAL'® AND 'TO-GIVE-AND-TO-KEEP'® ARE
REGISTERED TRADE MARKS OF EXLEY PUBLICATIONS LTD AND
EXLEY PUBLICATIONS LLC.

ACKNOWLEDGEMENTS: The publishers are grateful for permission to reproduce copyright
material. Whilst every reasonable effort has been made to trace copyright holders, the
publishers would be pleased to hear from any not here acknowledged. ANNE MORROW
LINDBERGH: From A Gift From The Sea, © Anne Morrow Lindbergh 1955, 1975, renewed
1983 by Anne Morrow Lindbergh. Published by Pantheon Books and Random House UK Ltd.
GLORIA NAYLOR: From Interviews with America's Writing Women by Mickey Pearlman and
Katherine V. Henderson. JOAN POWERS: From Eeyore's Gloomy Little Instruction Book,
inspired by A.A. Milne, written by Joan Powers. © 1996 Dutton Children's Books. ELEANOR
ROOSEVELT: From You Learn By Living, © 1960 E. Roosevelt, renewed 1988 Franklin A.
Roosevelt. Pam Brown, Carl Freeman, Joanna Jones and Helen Thomson © 1998.

To someone special
HAPPY BIRTHDAY

Edited by Helen Exley
Illustrated by Juliette Clarke

Happy birthday! It's time to
remember the good times that have
passed and to look forward to the
good times to come. I wish you
happiness today, and every day.

. . .

A HELEN EXLEY GIFTBOOK

EXLEY
NEW YORK • WATFORD, UK

IT'S YOUR BIRTHDAY!

It's your birthday, so let's call a toast:
Here's to health! Here's to happiness!
Here's to friendship! Here's to you!

…

Today is a special day to reflect on the past
years and the beautiful and growing
years ahead.

HELEN THOMSON, b.1943

May this birthday, this year, bring you more joy than the last, more peace than the last, more beauty and more comfort.

More freedom from the mundane cares of everyday life and more time to experience sweet moments of calm – may these gifts be yours today, and more.

CARL FREEMAN

. . .

You're special, so I hope that your birthday is special too!

I wish you brightly packaged gifts and greetings cards aplenty.

I wish you delicious food and drink and the companionship of friends.

I wish you surprises and celebrations, and the warmth of your family around you.

I wish you joy today and evermore.

Happy birthday!

JOANNA JONES

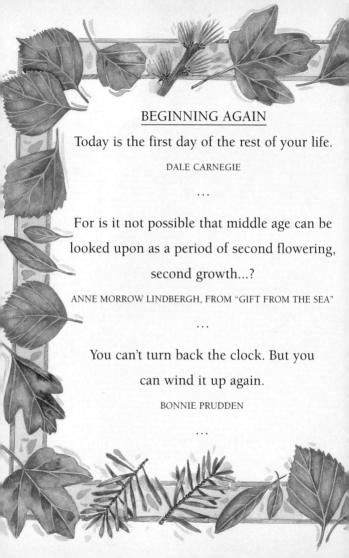

BEGINNING AGAIN

Today is the first day of the rest of your life.

DALE CARNEGIE

...

For is it not possible that middle age can be
looked upon as a period of second flowering,
second growth...?

ANNE MORROW LINDBERGH, FROM "GIFT FROM THE SEA"

...

You can't turn back the clock. But you
can wind it up again.

BONNIE PRUDDEN

...

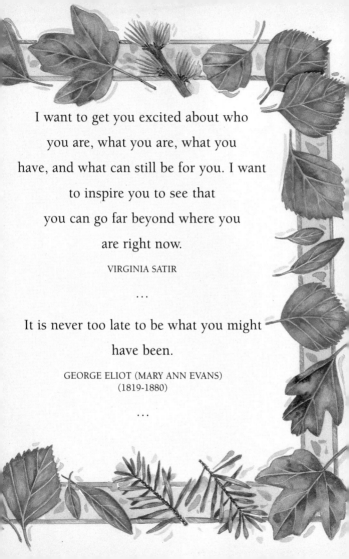

I want to get you excited about who
you are, what you are, what you
have, and what can still be for you. I want
to inspire you to see that
you can go far beyond where you
are right now.

VIRGINIA SATIR

...

It is never too late to be what you might
have been.

GEORGE ELIOT (MARY ANN EVANS)
(1819-1880)

...

TIME'S LITTLE TRICKS

Time is a dressmaker specializing in alterations.

FAITH BALDWIN

…

Just when you think no one has taken any notice of

your birthday, here come two friends with an empty

honey pot and a broken balloon.

JOAN POWERS, FROM "EEYORE'S GLOOMY LITTLE INSTRUCTION
BOOK, INSPIRED BY A.A. MILNE"

Experience: A comb life gives you after you
lose your hair.

JUDITH STERN

...

A man of forty today has nothing to worry him
but falling hair, inability to button the
top button, failing vision, shortness of breath,
a tendency of the collar to shut off all
breathing, trembling of the kidneys to whatever
tune the orchestra is playing, and a
general sense of giddiness when the matter of rent
is brought up. Forty is Life's Golden Age.

ROBERT BENCHLEY (1889-1945)

...

Life would be infinitely happier if we could only be
born at the age of eighty and
gradually approach eighteen.

MARK TWAIN (1835-1910)

...

DISCOVER YOURSELF

Discovering the ways in which you are exceptional,

the particular path you are

meant to follow, is your business on this earth...

It's just that the search takes

on a special urgency when you realize that

you are mortal.

BERNIE SIEGEL, M.D.

...

We neither get better or worse as we get older, but

more like ourselves.

ROBERT ANTHONY,
FROM "THINK AGAIN"

...

I began to have an idea of my life, not
as the slow shaping of achievement to fit my
preconceived purposes, but as the
gradual discovery and growth of a purpose
which I did not know.

JOANNA FIELD

...

You need to claim the events of your
life to make yourself yours. When you truly
possess all you have been and done,
which may take some time, you are
fierce with reality.

FLORIDA SCOTT-MAXWELL

...

I think of life itself now as a wonderful play that
I've written for myself... and so my purpose is to
have the utmost fun playing my part.

SHIRLEY MACLAINE, b.1934

...

YOUNG ALL YOUR LIFE

Youth is a state of the soul – nothing to do with age
– everything to do with attitude.

AUTHOR UNKNOWN

...

'Tis a maxim with me to be young as long as one
can: there is nothing can pay one for that invaluable
ignorance which is the companion of youth; those
sanguine groundless hopes, and that lively vanity,
which make all the happiness of life. To my extreme
mortification I grow wiser every day.

LADY MARY WORTLEY MONTAGU (1689-1762)

...

What can I say to you?
I am perhaps the oldest musician in the world.
I am an old man, but in many senses
a very young man. And this is what I want you
to be – young, young all your
life, and to say things to the world
that are true.

PABLO CASALS (1876-1973)

...

You were once wild here. Don't let them tame you!

ISADORA DUNCAN (1878-1927)

...

THE RAVAGES OF TIME

After thirty, a body has a mind of its own.

BETTE MIDLER, b.1945

...

I have everything I had twenty years ago, only it's
all a little bit lower.

GYPSY ROSE LEE

...

When I go to the beauty
parlor, I always use the
emergency entrance.
Sometimes I just go
for an estimate.

PHYLLIS DILLER, b.1917

Never forget – the reflection
in the shop window isn't you.
It's a trick of the light.

PAM BROWN, b.1928

Nightclubs used to seem so exciting,
with soft lights and champagne. But at 4 a.m. the
lights come on – there's a hole in the sofa,
and you notice the person you've been talking
to has yellow teeth.

PATSY KENSIT

...

Midlife crisis is that moment when
you realize your children and your clothes are
about the same age.

BILL TAMMEUS

...

He was at that time of life when a man
becomes aware of his plumbing, when he wakes
in the night to sounds of protest from
within – joints creaking, intestines in a riot.

PAUL BAILEY, FROM
"OLD SOLDIERS"

...

OPENING UP

At middle age the soul should be opening up like a rose, not closing up like a cabbage.

JOHN ANDREW HOLMES

…

I have enjoyed greatly the second blooming that comes when you finish the life of the emotions and of personal relations; and suddenly find... that a whole new life has opened before you.... It is as if a fresh sap of ideas and thoughts was rising in you.

AGATHA CHRISTIE (1890-1976)
FROM "AN AUTOBIOGRAPHY"

…

The belief that youth is the happiest time of life is founded on a fallacy. The happiest person is the person who thinks the most interesting thoughts, and we grow happier as we grow older.

WILLIAM LYON PHELPS

…

LIVE THE MOMENT

Life isn't a matter of milestones but
of moments.

ROSE FITZGERALD KENNEDY

...

We all grow up at last and lose that first
sharp vision of the world. We miss dew, sparkle,
leaf shadow, spider scuttle, puddle shine.
We waste time on worry.
And we find the days sweep by, each blurred,
each like the other.
Draw breath and rediscover little things.

PAM BROWN, b.1928

...

My heart leaps up when I behold

A rainbow in the sky:

So was it when my life began;

So it is now I am a man:

So be it when I shall grow old,

Or let me die!

WILLIAM WORDSWORTH (1770-1850)

...

Sometimes I would almost rather

have people take away years of my life than

take away a moment.

PEARL BAILEY

...

The gift from middle age

was the ability to enjoy the moment without

expecting it to last.

LISA ALTHER, b.1944,
FROM "OTHER WOMEN"

...

FREEDOM

And so what I've learned in the last twenty years is that I am the sole judge and jury about what my limits will be.

And as I look toward the horizon of the next twenty years, it is no... no limit. With that kind of knowledge, I've grown as old as I can possibly be; the aging has stopped here, and now I just grow better.

GLORIA NAYLOR

...

And then, not expecting it, you become middle-
aged and anonymous. No one notices you. You
achieve a wonderful freedom. It is a positive thing.
You can move about, unnoticed and invisible.

DORIS LESSING, b.1919

...

Risk! Risk anything!
Care no more for the opinion of others, for those
voices. Do the hardest thing on earth for you.
Act for yourself. Face the truth.

KATHERINE MANSFIELD (1888-1923)

...

Perhaps middle-age is, or should be, a period of
shedding shells; the shell of ambition, the
shell of material accumulations and possessions,
the shell of the ego.

ANNE MORROW LINDBERGH,
FROM "A GIFT FROM THE SEA"

...

CONTENT TO BE OUR AGE

I'm very pleased with each advancing year.
It stems back to when I was forty. I was a bit upset
about reaching that milestone,
but an older friend consoled me. "Don't
complain about growing old
– many people don't have that privilege."

EARL WARREN

...

One of the many things nobody ever tells
you about middle age is that it's such a nice change
from being young.

DOROTHY CANFIELD FISHER (1879-1958)

...

Live in each season as it passes, breathe the air,
drink the drink, taste the fruit, and resign yourself
to the influences of each.

HENRY DAVID THOREAU (1817-1862)

...

Life is what we make it, always has
been, always will be.

GRANDMA MOSES (1860-1961)

...

There is no cure for birth and death
save to enjoy the interval.

GEORGE SANTAYANA (1863-1952)

...

Why ape the young, when you have
gifts they still can only dream of?

PAM BROWN, b.1928

THE CHILDREN THAT WE WERE

When we were very small we played together under

the summer trees, picked dandelions to carry home,

drew in the dust of shadowed lanes, stamped in

mud, kicked joyfully through Autumn leaves.

Age was no concern of ours.

The seasons gave their gifts and gave no hint that

time would mark us.

But the trees are felled, the meadows vanished,

the lanes forgotten. And you and I

are growing middle-aged.

Walk with me then, and talk of those lost times –

still vivid in our minds. Still living in our hearts.

Life is still good – but we live in both worlds.

We recognize the children that we were shining

in one another's eyes.

And smile – knowing that nothing good is

ever lost.

PAM BROWN, b.1928

...

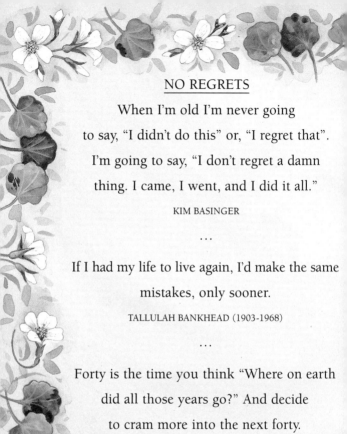

NO REGRETS

When I'm old I'm never going
to say, "I didn't do this" or, "I regret that".
I'm going to say, "I don't regret a damn
thing. I came, I went, and I did it all."

KIM BASINGER

...

If I had my life to live again, I'd make the same
mistakes, only sooner.

TALLULAH BANKHEAD (1903-1968)

...

Forty is the time you think "Where on earth
did all those years go?" And decide
to cram more into the next forty.

PAM BROWN, b.1928

Each of us has... all the time there is. Those years, weeks, hours, are the sands in the glass running swiftly away. To let them drift through our fingers is tragic waste. To use them to the hilt, making them count for something, is the beginning of wisdom.

ELEANOR ROOSEVELT (1884-1962)

I don't want to get to the end of my life and find that I lived just the length of it. I want to have lived the width of it as well.

DIANE ACKERMAN,
IN "NEWSWEEK"

...